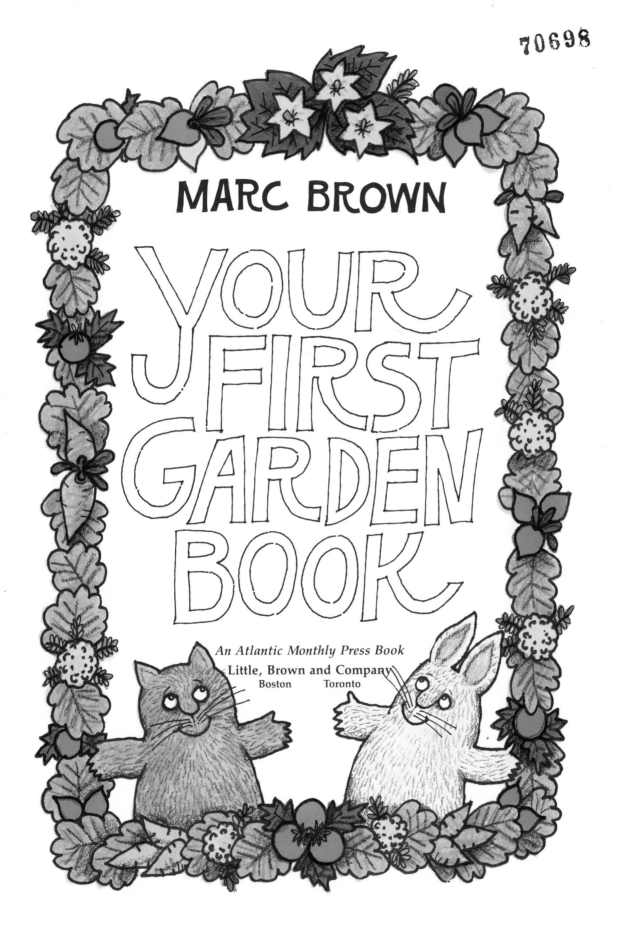

MARC BROWN

YOUR FIRST GARDEN BOOK

An Atlantic Monthly Press Book

Little, Brown and Company
Boston   Toronto

Also by Marc Brown
One Two Three
Arthur's Nose
Arthur's Eyes
Arthur's Valentine
The True Francine

For my Mom and Dad, who gave me a beautiful
place to grow — especially my Dad,
who shared his love of growing everything
from pachysandra to onion sandwiches

FIRST EDITION

Library of Congress Cataloging in Publication Data

Brown, Marc Tolon.
  Your first garden book.

  "An Atlantic Monthly Press book."
  Includes index.
  Summary: Suggested projects outline for beginning
gardeners how to sprout seeds, turn soil, plant,
and care for the results.
  1. Gardening — Juvenile literature. [1. Gardening]
I. Title.
SB457.B7   635   81–3681
ISBN 0–316–11217–8   AACR2
ISBN 0–316–11215–1 (pbk.)

ATLANTIC–LITTLE, BROWN BOOKS
ARE PUBLISHED BY
LITTLE, BROWN AND COMPANY
IN ASSOCIATION WITH
THE ATLANTIC MONTHLY PRESS

BP
*Published simultaneously in Canada
by Little, Brown & Company (Canada) Limited*

PRINTED IN THE UNITED STATES OF AMERICA

CONTENTS

MAGIC BEANS
See How Seeds Work

YOU WILL NEED:
several large dried lima beans (you can find them in a supermarket)
an empty pickle or jelly jar
paper towels
water

HOW TO DO IT:
1. Fill the jar with 2 or 3 paper towels.
2. Put the beans inside next to the glass.
3. Put about 1 inch of water in the jar to keep the towels moist.
4. Find a warm, dark place — like a linen closet.
5. In a few days you will see the seeds get bigger. Roots will appear. And then the first leaves.

GROW BEAN SPROUTS

YOU WILL NEED:
½ cup of mung beans (you can find them at health-food, hardware, or garden stores)
a quart-size screw-top jar
water

HOW TO DO IT:
1. Wash the beans and soak them in water overnight.
2. Drain off the water. (Use it to water your plants — it's good for them!)
3. Punch holes in the lid of your jar using a hammer and a nail.
4. Put in your beans and screw on the lid.
5. Put the jar in a dark place.
6. Rinse the beans 2 or 3 times a day.
7. The bean sprouts will be ready in just 5 days! They're great in salads or on sandwiches.

CRESS GARDEN IN A DISH

YOU WILL NEED:
2 plates
paper towel
1 pack of cress seeds (good for several crops; see page 44 for where to buy seeds)

HOW TO DO IT:

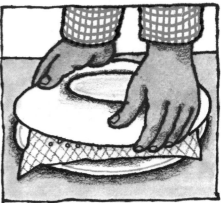

1. Put a paper towel on the plate.
2. Wet the towel well with water.
3. Sprinkle seeds on the wet towel.
4. Cover the seeds with another plate.
5. Check every day to make sure the paper is still moist.
6. When the cress is ½ inch high (about 3 days), uncover it and place the plate in a sunny window. Keep the paper moist.
7. When the cress is 3 inches high it's time to harvest it with scissors.

Enjoy your cress on a sandwich or in a salad. Delicious!

CRESS SANDWICHES TASTE BETTER BECAUSE YOU GROW THEM YOURSELF!

A DESERT GARDEN FOR LAZY GARDENERS

Pick out your favorite kinds of cacti. There are many weird ones with funny names.

Here are some kinds of cacti and other succulent plants: ➔

There are many more to choose from.

YOU WILL NEED:
cacti — about 4 or 5 varieties
a flat dish or tray
maybe a rocket ship or doll or toy
sand or gravel

HOW TO DO IT:
1. Keep each cactus in its pot. The roots like to be in small pots.
2. Arrange potted cacti in the dish. Fill the dish with sand or gravel to keep the pots in place. Add something strange like a rocket for a moonscape.
3. Every week the cacti need a little warm (not hot) water.
4. Keep your cacti out of drafts but in the sun.

WHAT DID THE BABY PORCUPINE SAY TO THE CACTUS?

MOMMY, IS THAT YOU?

BUNNY EARS

ZEBRA HAWORTHIA

JELLY BEANS

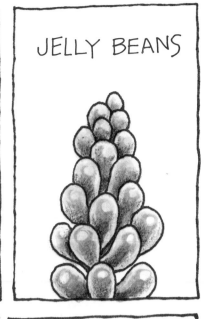

OLD MAN

PAINTED LADY

RAT'S TAIL

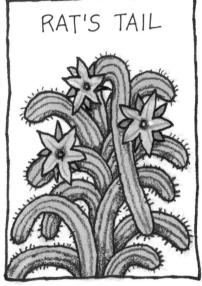

TIGER'S JAWS

MOONSTONES

WART PLANT

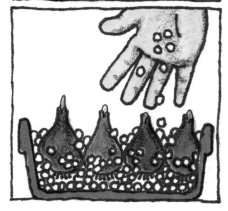

GROWING BULBS INDOORS

With bulbs you can have flowers in your house from October to spring. Some of the easiest bulbs to grow are paperwhite narcissus, hyacinths, and crocuses. They make great Christmas gifts, too!

Paperwhite Narcissus

YOU WILL NEED:
3–6 bulbs (see page 45 for where to buy them)
shallow dish or bowl
pebbles, gravel, or sand

HOW TO DO IT:
1. Put half the pebbles or sand in the dish.
2. Arrange the bulbs — roots down and close together.
3. Add enough sand or pebbles to cover the bottom half of the bulbs (the tops of the bulbs should show).
4. Place the dish in a cool, sunny window.
5. Always keep the roots wet.

You will have flowers in about 4 weeks — they smell great! If you want flowers for Christmas, plant your bulbs two weeks before Thanksgiving.

IF YOU CUT A HYACINTH BULB IN HALF YOU'LL SEE THE BEGINNING HYACINTH PLANT WITH ITS SMALL LEAVES AND FLOWER BUDS.

INSIDE A HYACINTH BULB

LEAVES

FLOWER BUD

FOOD

Crocuses or Hyacinths

YOU WILL NEED:

3–6 bulbs especially treated for forcing
   indoors
small pot or cup
soil (any kind is fine)

HOW TO DO IT:

1. Fill the pot ¾ full with soil.
2. Arrange bulbs, points up.
3. Add more soil until only the tips of the bulbs show.
4. Place the pot in a cool, sunny window.
5. Keep the soil moist.

Crocus flowers will open in about 4 weeks, hyacinths in 4–6 weeks.

HYACINTHS WILL PROBABLY NEED STAKES AFTER THE FLOWERS OPEN.

THE FLYING MONSTER PLANT

YOU WILL NEED:

a piece of sponge (the natural kind, not
man-made) from the hardware store
string
birdseed (or mustard, grass, cress, clover,
or rye seeds)
dish of water
2 cardboard circles the size of a quarter
2 toothpicks

HOW TO DO IT:

1. Tie the string around the sponge. Leave
one long end.
2. Soak the sponge in water.
3. Sprinkle the seeds onto the sponge.
4. Stick the toothpicks through the cardboard circles to make monster eyes.
5. Now stick the eyes into the sponge.
6. Hang the sponge in a sunny window.
7. Soak the sponge in water every day.

Now watch your monster grow long
green hair!

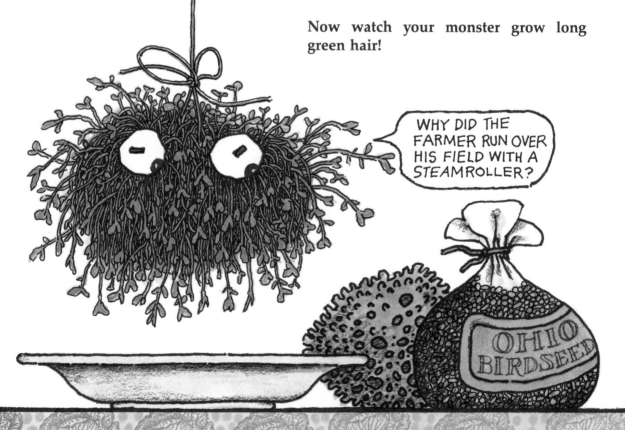

WHY DID THE FARMER RUN OVER HIS FIELD WITH A STEAMROLLER?

OHIO BIRDSEED

POTATOES IN A BUCKET

YOU WILL NEED:
a large bucket with holes in the bottom
   for drainage (a plastic wash bucket or
   wastebasket works well)
a potato with lots of eyes
soil and a little fertilizer
stones
water

HOW TO DO IT:
1. Let the potato sit in a light, airy place
   for about 2 weeks. Sprouts will grow
   out of its eyes.
2. Snap off all but the two strongest
   sprouts.
3. Cover the bottom of the bucket with
   stones.
4. Fill half the bucket with soil. Mix in
   3 handfuls of fertilizer.
5. Bury the potato in the soil. Keep the
   soil damp.
6. New shoots will appear in 3 or 4 weeks.
   Cover them with more soil. Potatoes are
   forming underground!
7. As more new shoots appear, cover them
   with soil until the bucket is full. Remember to keep the soil damp.
8. Soon you will see flowers. When they
   die, stop watering. When the whole
   plant dies (in about 4 months), tip over
   the bucket and count your potatoes!

BECAUSE HE WANTED TO RAISE MASHED POTATOES!

THE GLORIOUS GARBAGE GARDEN

Fruit and vegetable scraps that might end up in the garbage can blossom into a beautiful garden. Here's how to make it happen.

Avocado

YOU WILL NEED:

an avocado seed
a small jar with an opening a little wider than the avocado seed
3 or 4 toothpicks
soil
small pot

HOW TO DO IT:

1. Push toothpicks into the middle of the seed.
2. Set the seed on the mouth of the jar, pointed end up.
3. Put enough water in the jar to cover the bottom half of the seed.
4. When roots and leaves appear, plant the seed in soil in a small pot.
5. Place the pot in a sunny window.
6. Keep the soil damp.

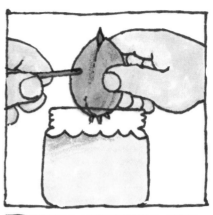

PINCH OFF THESE SMALL LEAVES ON THE TOP TO MAKE YOUR AVOCADO BRANCH OUT.

12

Orange, Grapefruit, Tangerine, and Lemon Trees

YOU WILL NEED:

orange, grapefruit, tangerine, or lemon
  seeds
several pots filled with potting soil

HOW TO DO IT:

1. Rinse the seeds and dry them in a paper
   towel.
2. Fill small pots with potting soil — one
   pot for each kind of seed you want to
   try.
3. With your finger, make a hole 3 inches
   deep for each seed (3 per pot). Put a
   seed in each hole and gently tap the dirt
   to cover the seed. It's a good idea to
   label each pot.
4. Put the pots in a warm, dark place and
   water them every day.
5. When shoots appear, move the pots to a
   sunny window.
6. Keep the soil moist.

Carrots, Turnips, Beets, and Parsnips

YOU WILL NEED:

tops of a few root vegetables
a plate or shallow dish
water

HOW TO DO IT:

1. Trim off any leaves.
2. Cut 1 inch off the top of each vegetable.
3. Put the tops on a plate. Add just
   enough water to cover the bottom of the
   plate.
4. Place the plate in a sunny window. In a
   few days, new shoots will appear.
5. Keep your plants well watered and in 2
   or 3 weeks you'll have a very leafy
   garden!

13

Pineapples

YOU WILL NEED:

a very warm place, because pineapples grow naturally in hot places

a pineapple

a pot of sand (with drainage holes)

CUT ← HERE

HOW TO DO IT:

1. Cut the top off the pineapple, leaving only 1 inch of fruit.
2. Let the top dry on its side for 5 days.
3. Plant it in a pot of damp sand. Bury the fruit part completely but leave the green leaves uncovered.
4. Set the pot in a warm, sunny place. Keep the sand damp but not too wet.
5. In 2 or 3 months, when roots have developed, transfer the plant to a pot with potting soil.
6. Keep the soil moist and you will have a beautiful plant. If you want to grow pineapple fruit, you will need a lot of patience (it takes 2–3 years) and a tropical climate or greenhouse.

PRESIDENTIAL PEANUT PLANT

You can grow this anytime, but if you want to harvest peanuts, start on George Washington's birthday (February 22), plant outside on John F. Kennedy's birthday (May 29), and you will have peanuts by Jimmy Carter's birthday (October 1).

YOU WILL NEED:
paper towel
1 jelly jar
6–8 shelled, unroasted peanuts
6-to-12-inch pot with a hole in the bottom
potting soil

HOW TO DO IT:
1. Wet the paper towel and put it in the jelly jar.
2. Tuck the peanuts around the edge between the glass and the paper towel. Don't let them sit on the bottom.
3. Keep the paper towel moist. You should see roots in 2 days.
4. When the strongest plant is 3 inches tall, carefully move it to a small pot filled with potting soil. Hold the plant by the leaves, not by the stem.
5. Make a hole in the soil. Gently lower the roots into the hole and cover them with soil.
6. Place the pot in a sunny window and keep the soil moist.
7. The peanuts grow under the soil, and should be ready to dig up in 4 months!

GEORGE WASHINGTON CARVER FOUND OVER 300 USES FOR THE PEANUT PLANT INCLUDING CHEESE, MILK, COFFEE, FLOUR, INK, DYES, SOAP, WOOD STAINS, AND INSULATION!

THE GIANT SUNFLOWER RACE

Sunflowers grow very, very fast! Why not have a race with your friends to see who can grow the tallest flower? Start your race on the first day of summer vacation and pick the winner on the last day. Decide on prizes now!

YOU WILL NEED:

giant sunflower seeds (*Helianthus*) — buy 1 pack and divide seeds among your friends

water

a sunny spot outdoors

HOW TO DO IT:

1. Plant seeds ½ inch deep and 3 feet apart.
2. Water every day.

AFTER THE FLOWER HAS BLOOMED THE CENTER SEEDS WILL TURN BLACK.
YOU CAN EAT THESE!
THEY TASTE LIKE NUTS.
CRACK THE OUTSIDE WITH YOUR TEETH AND EAT THE INSIDE.
BIRDS, HAMSTERS, AND GERBILS LOVE THEM!
SUNFLOWER SEEDS MAKE GREAT GIFTS. PUT THEM IN A JAR, TIE A RIBBON AROUND IT, AND MAKE A LABEL.

FOR THE BIRDS

Birds help keep unwanted insects out of your garden, so be good to them.

High-Rise Restaurant

YOU WILL NEED:
1-quart milk carton
stick about 12 inches long
a few small rocks
scissors or knife
strong string
pencil
birdseed

HOW TO DO IT:
1. Cut openings in the milk carton as shown. Leave enough space at the bottom for the stick perch.
2. With the pencil poke 5 small holes in the bottom for drainage. The holes must be smaller than the birdseed!
3. Poke the stick through the carton. Leave the same length on each side for a perch.
4. Put small rocks in the bottom of the carton.
5. With the pencil make a hole for string at the very top.
6. Fill the bottom of the carton with birdseed.
7. Hang the carton from a sturdy branch.

PUT SEED HERE

BIRDS LOVE PEANUT BUTTER AND SUNFLOWER SEEDS. TRY PUTTING SOME ON A PINECONE AND HANGING IT IN A TREE!

STRING SOME PEANUTS AND POPCORN FOR THE BIRDS

U.F.O. (Unidentified Feeding Object)

YOU WILL NEED:

large pie tin
small pie tin
screw eye
7 inches of a broom handle or wooden
    dowel
jar lid
nail and hammer
strong string
birdseed

HOW TO DO IT:

1. Nail the small pie tin, with the jar lid underneath for support, to the bottom of the broom handle.
2. Use the screw eye to attach the large pie tin to the top of the 7-inch piece of broom handle.
3. Fill the bottom of the U.F.O. with bird-seed.
4. Attach one end of the string to the screw eye and the other end to a strong branch.

Bird House
(colonial model shown)

YOU WILL NEED:

plastic bleach bottle (wash out very well)
strong string for hanging
permanent marker
sharp knife
a few small rocks for weight

HOW TO DO IT:

1. Decorate the bottle with the permanent marker.
2. Cut a small opening for the door.
3. Using the knife, make small holes at the top for string.
4. Put rocks in the bottom for weight.
5. Now attach the string, tie the other end to a good tree with a strong branch, and wait for your new neighbors to move in!

SCREW EYE

BROOM HANDLE → OR DOWEL

PUT SEED HERE

← JAR LID

NAIL

HAVE AN ADULT HELP WITH THE KNIFE.

CRACK GARDEN

YOU WILL NEED:
a crack or small spot of soil along the
   sidewalk
an old spoon or fork
seeds
water

HOW TO DO IT:
1. Loosen soil with the fork or spoon.
2. Make holes as deep as your fingernail
   about 6 inches apart (check spacing and
   depth on seed package).
3. Plant 1 seed in each hole.
4. Water lightly every day. Water more
   heavily when leaves appear.

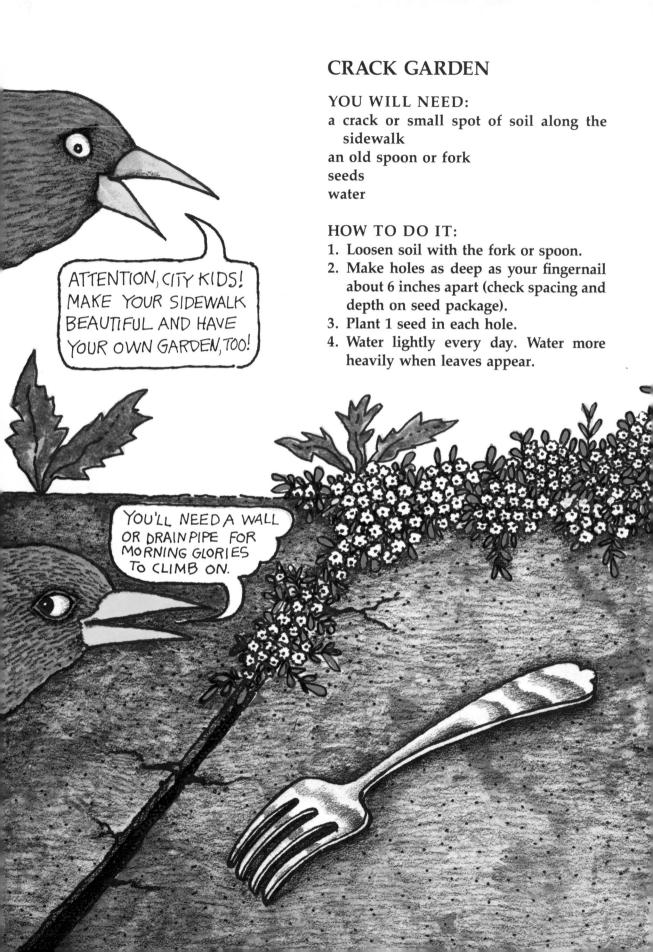

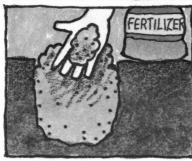

PLANT A PERFECT PUMPKIN

YOU WILL NEED:
Big Max pumpkin seeds

compost (see Super Soil, page 39) or commercial fertilizer or aged manure

a shovel

a sunny spot with a lot of room around it

HOW TO DO IT:
1. Dig a hole about a foot deep.
2. Mix the soil with a shovelful of compost or manure or 3 handfuls of fertilizer.
3. Pile the mixture loosely back into the hole.
4. Make the soil into a small mound about 18 inches across.
5. With your finger make 3 holes in the mound. Plant 1 seed in each hole.
6. Gently pat down the soil. Water every day.
7. When the plants are 6 inches high, choose the best plant on the mound and pull out the rest.
8. The vine will produce blossoms, then the blossoms will produce small pumpkins. When you have 3 pumpkins on the vine, pick off any new blossoms.
9. Pinch off the fuzzy ends of the vine. This will make your pumpkins larger.
10. When the stems are dry the pumpkins are ready to pick.

PUMPKINS FORM AT THE BASE OF THE FEMALE FLOWER

PUMPKIN FACT
14-YEAR-OLD ROBERT TAYLOR FROM MARIETTA, GEORGIA, GREW A 230-POUND PUMPKIN. IT WON FIRST PRIZE IN THE MEN'S GARDEN CLUB OF AMERICA BIG PUMPKIN CONTEST.

PUMPKINS TAKE 4 MONTHS. PLANT IN JUNE TO BE IN TIME FOR HALLOWEEN.

HOMEGROWN HALLOWEEN

The Great Jack-O'-Lantern Contest

1. Challenge your friends to a pumpkin race.
2. Declare 1 mound as your territory. Have each contestant do the same.
3. Make a flag with your name on it to mark your mound.
4. Plant and grow your pumpkin seeds as described on pages 22 and 23.
5. Weigh your best pumpkins on the bathroom scale.
6. The heaviest pumpkin wins!

Now have a jack-o'-lantern contest to see who can carve the best faces. Give awards for the funniest, scariest, craziest.

Roasted Pumpkin Seeds
A great snack or treat for Halloween.

1. Wash the seeds well in a colander.
2. Dry in a paper towel.
3. Spread on a greased cookie sheet.
4. Bake in a 300° oven for 5 or 10 minutes,
   turning 2 or 3 times with a spatula.
5. Salt lightly. Eat while warm.
6. Or put in small bags for treats.

HOLIDAY HARVEST

Catnip Pillow
The perfect gift for your favorite cat.

YOU WILL NEED:
yarn
large needle with eye big enough for yarn
cloth scrap, about 6 inches by 12 inches
cookie cutter
pencil
scissors
dried catnip
marker
small bell

HOW TO DO IT:
1. Fold the cloth in half.
2. With the pencil, trace around the cookie cutter on one side of the cloth. That will be the shape of your pillow.
3. Cut out through both layers of cloth, following your pencil mark.
4. With yarn and needle, sew the two halves together. Leave a 1-inch opening.
5. Stuff the pillow with catnip through the small opening.
6. Now, sew up the opening.
7. Sew on the bell and add a face with the marker.

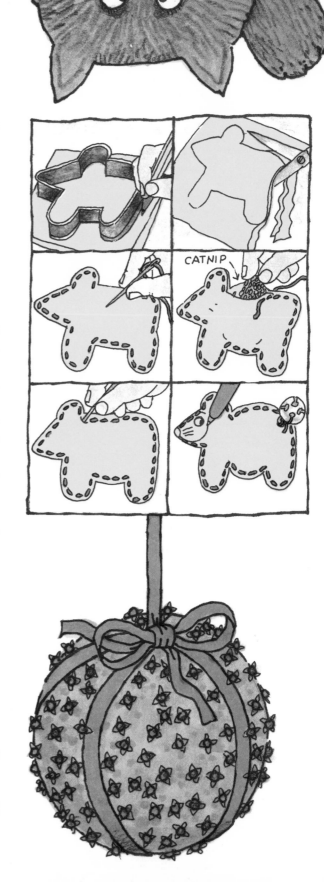

CATNIP

Super Smells
Simple stocking stuffers.

YOU WILL NEED:
1 orange, apple, lemon, or lime
whole cloves
ribbon or yarn

HOW TO DO IT:
1. Push the cloves into the fruit. Cover the whole fruit with cloves.
2. Tie ribbon or yarn around the fruit.
3. Hang anywhere you want a super smell!

Seeds for Someone Special

These make great holiday gifts for your hamster or gerbil, too!

YOU WILL NEED:
your dried sunflower or pumpkin seeds
small jar
paper and glue or self-sticking labels
markers
ribbon

HOW TO DO IT:
1. On your paper or labels, draw a pretty design.
2. Glue this onto the jar.
3. Fill the jar with your dried seeds.
4. Tie a ribbon around the jar.

Potato-Print Paper

Make your own holiday cards, gift and name tags, and wrapping paper.

YOU WILL NEED:
potato
small sharp knife
newspapers to work on
brush
watercolors or tempera paints
papers to print on (shelf paper, brown wrapping paper, and paper bags are fine)
pencil

HOW TO DO IT:
1. Cut the potato in half.
2. Use the pencil to draw a design on the potato.
3. Cut away any part of the potato that isn't in your design. The part you want to print should stand up about ¼ inch.
4. Brush paint on your design.
5. Print your design by pressing the potato on the paper.

EXPERIMENT WITH DIFFERENT COLORS. YOU HAVE TO ADD MORE PAINT TO THE POTATO AFTER EACH PRINT.
YOU CAN ALSO USE APPLES.

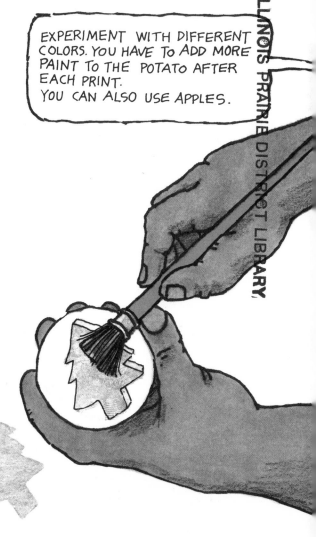

STARTING SEEDS INDOORS

YOU WILL NEED:
seeds — whatever kind you want to grow
egg cartons or milk cartons
pencil
potting soil
sand or vermiculite
a sunny window
water

HOW TO DO IT:

1. Cut the egg carton or milk carton as shown.
2. With the pencil, poke small holes in the bottom of the containers to let out excess water.
3. Mix the soil. The best soil for starting seeds is ½ sand or vermiculite and ½ potting soil.
4. Follow instructions on the seed packages for planting.
5. Label the containers with the plant names.
6. Place the pots in a sunny window.
7. Keep the soil moist. A plant sprayer is good for this.
8. When baby plants are large enough — 2 or 3 inches tall — you can replant them in pots so they have room to grow. Be careful moving them — use a butter knife or Popsicle stick to loosen the soil and help lift them out. Hold the plants gently by their leaves, not their stems!
9. Fill the pots with potting soil. Use a pencil to make holes for the plants in their new home.
10. Keep the soil moist.

WHEN SEEDLINGS HAVE TWO SETS OF LEAVES THEY ARE READY TO BE REPLANTED

THE FIRST 2 LEAVES ARE CALLED HEART LEAVES

USE YOUR OLD POPSICLE STICKS FOR LABELS

MINT

PLANT SPRA

FOR INDO
AND OUTD

PARSLEY

MINT

28

WINDOW HERB GARDEN

YOU WILL NEED:
small containers (almost anything works, from teacups to egg cartons)
tray or pan with small pebbles on the bottom
sand or vermiculite
potting soil
seeds

HERBS THAT GROW BEST INDOORS:

Chives	Parsley
Caraway	Thyme
Dill	Mint
Sweet Basil	Sage
Fennel	Anise
Catnip	Marjoram

Seed catalogues may list other herbs you'd like to try. There are enough seeds in most packages to share with 2 or 3 friends.

DWARF TOMATOES ARE ANOTHER GOOD THING TO GROW ON YOUR WINDOWSILL!

HOW TO DO IT:
Follow the directions on individual seed packages for planting. But remember to:

1. Keep your pots in a pan with 1 inch of pebbles on the bottom. Put the pan in a sunny window.
2. Water the pots whenever the soil becomes dry. Add enough water to cover the pebbles.
3. Harvest by cutting off the tips with scissors when the plants are 4 or 5 inches high.

Herbs grow quickly if you keep cutting!

HERB-DRYING TIPS
1. Pick branches of the herbs when the plants are flowering.
2. Tie them in small bunches. (Use rubber bands — they get tighter as the herbs dry.) Hang them upside down in a warm place to dry.
3. When the herbs are dry, they will crumble in your hands. Store the herbs in airtight glass containers. They make great gifts for people who enjoy cooking!

VEGETABLES FOR CITY GARDENS

Just because you live in the city doesn't mean you can't grow vegetables. All you need is a sunny spot on a roof, fire escape, porch, or in a parking lot or window box. Plan what you want to grow. Here are some of the things that grow best in containers in the city:

Cherry Tomatoes	Carrots
Peppers	Beets
Lettuce	Herbs
Radishes	Cucumbers
Onions	

You can even grow pumpkins in a large container.

THOMAS JEFFERSON WAS THE FIRST PERSON IN AMERICA TO GROW TOMATOES. HE USED THEM AS DECORATION IN HIS GARDEN, NOT TO EAT.

YOU WILL NEED:

a sunny place

containers — see page 34 for ideas. (Be sure to make small drainage holes in the bottoms of your containers. You can use a can opener or hammer and nail to do this.)

water

potting soil

seeds

HOW TO DO IT:

Check each seed package for individual planting directions.

Hints:

1. When gardening in containers you must water them each day.
2. Plants in pots need extra food. Every 2 weeks, serve them some commercial plant food with their water.

WHAT DO YOU GET WHEN YOU CROSS A TOMATO WITH A GORILLA?

A TOMATO NOBODY PICKS ON!

IDEAL CONTAINERS FOR CITY GARDENS

TIN CANS—LIKE
SOUP OR COFFEE
CANS

MILK AND
JUICE CARTONS

OLD PIE, CAKE, OR
MUFFIN TINS

GLASS JARS
PAPER CUPS

ICE CREAM CONTAINERS

OLD SHOES

SHOE BOXES

SEASHELLS
EGGSHELLS

BLEACH BOTTLES —
HAVE AN ADULT CUT OFF
THE TOP, THEN WASH
OUT VERY WELL

BUSHEL AND PECK BASKETS

FISHBOWLS

CLAY POTS
PLASTIC POTS
OLD DRAWERS

PLASTIC BUCKETS
WASTE BASKETS
DISH PANS

GARDEN TOOLS

HAND TROWEL FOR PLANTING AND DIGGING SMALL HOLES

WATERING CAN AND HOSE FOR WATERING YOUR GARDEN

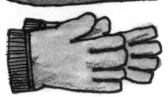

SHOVEL FOR DIGGING UP THE EARTH

YOU MIGHT WANT TO WEAR SOME OLD GLOVES

SPADING FORK FOR DIGGING AND BREAKING UP LUMPS IN THE SOIL

HOE FOR BREAKING UP CLUMPS OF SOIL AND WEEDING

RAKE FOR CLEARING AND EVENING THE SOIL

YOU MIGHT NEED A HAT ON VERY SUNNY DAYS

Alternative Tools

HOMEMADE RAKE: EASY TO MAKE FROM 2 PIECES OF WOOD AND 10 LONG NAILS

MARK OFF A YARDSTICK ON THE HANDLE →

OLD FORK FOR DIGGING

OLD SPOON FOR DIGGING

SHOEHORN FOR DIGGING HOLES

STRONG STICK FOR DIGGING HOLES, MARKING ROWS, AND PLANTING SEEDS

FIND THE GARDEN GOOD GUYS

Be nice to these creatures!
They will help your garden.

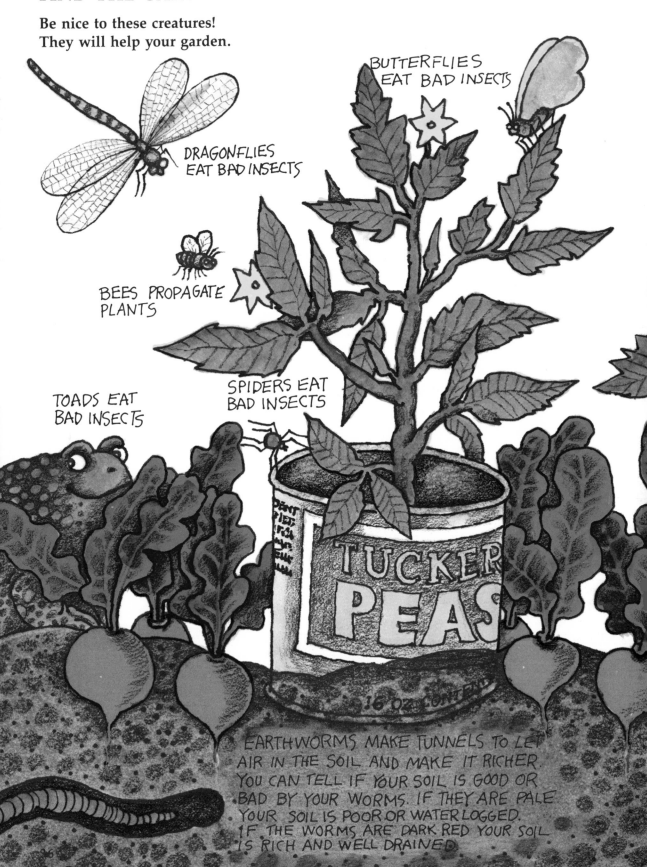

BUTTERFLIES
EAT BAD INSECTS

DRAGONFLIES
EAT BAD INSECTS

BEES PROPAGATE
PLANTS

SPIDERS EAT
BAD INSECTS

TOADS EAT
BAD INSECTS

TUCKER
PEAS

16 OZ CONTEND

EARTHWORMS MAKE TUNNELS TO LET
AIR IN THE SOIL AND MAKE IT RICHER.
YOU CAN TELL IF YOUR SOIL IS GOOD OR
BAD BY YOUR WORMS. IF THEY ARE PALE
YOUR SOIL IS POOR OR WATER LOGGED.
IF THE WORMS ARE DARK RED YOUR SOIL
IS RICH AND WELL DRAINED

PRAYING MANTISES
EAT BAD INSECTS

LADYBUGS
EAT
APHIDS

SOME BIRDS EAT
BAD INSECTS AND
BOTH GOOD AND BAD
SEEDS

SNAKES EAT
BAD INSECTS

MARIGOLDS MAKE
GREAT GARDEN
GUARDS-THE
STRONG ODOR
KEEPS PESTS
AWAY

A COUNTRY GARDEN

HOW TO DO IT:

1. Choose your seeds.
2. Check the seed packages for any special directions.
3. Plan the arrangement of your garden by making a map.
4. Choose a sunny spot (3 feet by 4 feet is a good size).
5. Clear away any rocks and pull out all weeds by the roots.
6. Use a shovel or spading fork to turn over the soil. Make sure to dig up all the space (about 8 inches deep) and break up all lumps of dirt.
7. Sprinkle compost, composted manure, or commercial fertilizer on the area and mix into the soil. (See Super Soil.)
8. Rake the soil.
9. Find some stakes or sticks to mark off straight rows. Put a stick in each corner (after measuring with a yardstick) and connect the sticks with string.
10. Mark off the end of each row (rows are usually about 12 inches apart) with more sticks and connect them with string as shown. This will keep your rows straight.
11. Using your shovel, make trenches 3 inches deep under the string.
12. Now plant your seeds, covering them lightly with dirt. Water every day.

Super Soil

Compost is rich organic matter. When you add it to the soil it helps plants grow. Use it for your gardens indoors and out as an extra boost.

To recycle waste and make compost, or super soil:

1. Dig a hole about 3 feet wide and 2 to 3 feet deep.
2. In the hole make layers of plant matter (vegetable scraps, grass clippings, and leaves) and soil. It will become rich compost as the plant matter decays.
3. Check the hole now and then. When the leaves and grass clippings have completely disappeared, dig in with your shovel and mix up the layers. Your compost is now ready to use!

GROW A SALAD

Radishes

1. Choose your radish. There are red ones or white.
2. Plant seeds ½ inch deep. Space them 2 inches apart. Rows should be 10 inches apart.
3. Water each day.
4. In a few days, leaves will appear. Thin plants so that their leaves are 2 inches apart (this means pulling out extra plants).
5. In 3 weeks, your radishes will be ready to pull up and eat. You can plant 4 crops, one after another, from spring until fall.

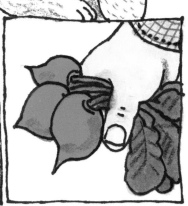

Carrots

1. Plant in rows 12 inches apart.
2. Seeds are very small and should be planted ¼ inch deep and thinned to 6 inches apart when plants are 3 inches high.
3. Carrots take longer, 65–75 days. Be patient and keep watering them each day.
4. When the orange carrot tops are ½ inch wide — harvest!

Lettuce

Bibb lettuce is an easy lettuce to grow.

1. Make rows 15–18 inches apart.
2. Plant seeds ½ inch deep and 1–2 inches apart.
3. Water each day.
4. When plants are 2 inches high, thin them out to 6 inches apart.
5. Your lettuce will be ready to pick in 45–50 days.

MORE EASY THINGS YOU MIGHT WANT TO TRY IN YOUR FIRST GARDEN ARE: PEAS, BEANS, BEETS, SQUASH, ONIONS, SCALLIONS, HERBS, AND SPINACH.

BIBB LETTUCE

☆ START WITH SMALL PLANTS FROM THE NURSERY. YOU'LL NEED ONLY 3 OR 4 PLANTS. MOSTLY THEY COME 6 IN A FLAT, SO YOU CAN SHARE WITH A FRIEND.

WHEN YOU PLANT, PUT A CAN (OPEN AT BOTH ENDS) AROUND EACH PLANT. THIS WILL KEEP CUTWORMS AWAY.

SHUCKS!

You can add to your salad by also growing cucumber and tomato plants.

Tomatoes

1. Pick your spot. Tomatoes need lots of sun.
2. Loosen the soil and plant the tomatoes 2–3 feet apart.
3. Water each day.
4. When the plants are 1 foot high, put a stake or strong stick next to each one. Tie the plant to the stake so it will stand up.

WHAT'S RED AND GOES BEEP, BEEP, SLAM, SLAM, SLAM, SLAM?

A 4-DOOR TOMATO IN A TRAFFIC JAM.

Cucumbers

Cucumbers need a lot of room, so plant only 1 or 2 mounds. You can start them from seeds like pumpkins, or buy small plants from a nursery.

1. Plant in late spring or early summer in small mounds 3 feet apart.
2. Plant 5 or 6 seeds per mound.
3. Water each day.
4. When plants are 4 inches high, thin out all but the best 2 or 3 plants. (If you start with nursery plants, put 2 in a mound.)
5. Don't let your cucumbers get too big — they won't taste as good!

WHERE TO FIND GARDEN BASICS

Seeds

Think spring in winter! Send for free seed catalogues and plan your garden.

Check seed displays at supermarkets, five-and-tens, hardware and garden stores. If you don't find the seeds you want, you can find them in seed catalogues. Try to pick a seed company nearby because they will have seeds that grow best in your area.

Where to Send:

1. Allen, Sterling & Lathrop
191 U.S. Route #1
Falmouth, Maine 04105

2. Chas. C. Hart Seed Company
304 Main Street
Wethersfield, Connecticut 06109

3. Stokes Seeds
737 Main
Buffalo, New York 14240

4. Seedway
Hall, New York 14463

5. Joseph Harris Company
3670 Buffalo Road
Rochester, New York 14624

6. Burpee Seed Company
300 Park Avenue
Warminster, Pennsylvania 19132

7. D. Landreth Seed Company
2700 Wilmarco Avenue
Baltimore, Maryland 21223

8. George Tait & Sons
900 Tidewater Drive
Norfolk, Virginia 23504

9. G. W. Park Seed Company
Greenwood, South Carolina 29646

10. H. G. Hastings Company
Box 4008
Atlanta, Georgia 30302

11. Glecklers Seedmen
Meadow Lane
Metamora, Ohio 43540

12. Burgess Seed & Plant Company
Box 3001
Galesburg, Michigan 49053

13. Henry Field Seed & Nursery Company
407 Sycamore Street
Shenandoah, Iowa 51601

14. J. W. Jung Seed Company
355 High Street
Randolph, Wisconsin 53956

15. Farmer Seed & Nursery Company
818 Fourth Street N.W.
Fair Bault, Minnesota 55021

16. Gurney Seed & Nursery Company
1448 Page Street
Yankton, South Dakota 57078

17. Reuter Seed Company
320 North Carrollton Avenue
New Orleans, Louisiana 70119

18. Robert Nicholson Seed Company
2700 Logan
Dallas, Texas 75215

19. Rocky Mountain Seed Company
1325 Fifteenth Street
Denver, Colorado 80217

20. Roswell Seed Company
115 South Main
Roswell, New Mexico 88201

21. J. L. Hudson
P.O. Box 1058
Redwood City, California 94064

22. Jackson & Perkins
2518 South Pacific Highway
Medford, Oregon 97501

23. Vesey's Seed Ltd.
York, Prince Edward Island
Canada

24. W. H. Perron & Company, Ltd.
515 Labelle Boulevard
Chomedey, Quebec
Canada

25. Ritchie Feed & Seed Ltd.
27 York Street
Ottawa, Ontario
Canada

Soil

Potting soil is good to use because it provides minerals that help plants make food. You can find it at dime stores, garden and hardware stores, and sometimes at supermarkets.

Fertilizers

Fertilizer is extra food for your plants. There are natural kinds, like compost and animal manures, or chemical kinds sold at hardware and garden-supply stores. Package directions will tell you how much to use.

Plant Food

Plant food comes in liquid and powder forms. You add it to the water you give your plants. It's important to follow the package directions. Plant food is sold in hardware, garden, and dime stores and in supermarkets.

Bulbs

Bulbs are sold by florists, in garden or hardware stores, or you can order them by mail.

Where to Send for Free Bulb Catalogues:

John Messelaar Bulb Company
Box 269
Ipswich, Massachusetts 01938

John Scheepers Inc.
63 H Wall Street
New York, New York 10005

Burpee Seed Company
(Ask for free bulb catalogue)
840 Burpee Building
Warminster, Pennsylvania 18974

Burpee Seed Company
Clinton, Iowa 52732

Burpee Seed Company
Riverside, California 92502

A GARDENER'S GLOSSARY

APHID: A tiny insect that sucks the juices from the shoots and leaves of plants.

BLOSSOM: See FLOWER.

BULB: A flower bud wrapped in thick leaves that provide food until the plant is able to grow in the soil. Many spring flowers, such as hyacinths and daffodils, grow from bulbs.

CACTUS: A family of fleshy desert plants with scales or spines instead of leaves. Their thick stems and branches hold supplies of water.

COMPOST: A fertilizer that is a rich mixture of soil and vegetable matter.

CUTWORM: A gray caterpillar that mows down small plants by chewing through their stems, then eats their leaves and buds.

DAMP: Slightly wet. To keep soil damp, give it only a little water at a time—just enough so that the soil doesn't dry out.

DRAINAGE: An escape route for excess water in a potted plant. Pebbles, pieces of broken pottery, or holes in the bottom of a pot provide good drainage.

FERTILIZER: Anything added to the soil to make it richer and to give plants more food.

FLAT: A shallow box in which small plants are grown from seeds. Plants are often sold by nurseries in flats of 6 or 12.

FLOWER: The cluster of organs and special leaves (petals), often brightly colored, by which some plants reproduce.

FORCING: Making plants blossom or bear fruit out of season by growing them indoors.

GREENHOUSE: A glass enclosure that lets sunshine reach the plants inside, but protects them from the cold outside air.

LEAF: A flat structure growing out from the stem of a plant that turns sunlight into food.

MANURE: Refuse from stables or barnyards that is used as fertilizer.

MOIST: See DAMP.

NURSERY: A place where shrubs, trees, and small plants for flowers and vegetables are grown.

ORGANIC: Made from things that are, or once were, alive rather than from chemicals or man-made materials.

PLANT FOOD: A liquid or powder fertilizer that can be added to the water given to potted plants.

POTTING SOIL: A special soil for potted plants that is sold in bags.

PROPAGATE: To help a kind of plant reproduce and spread in a garden. Bees propagate plants by carrying pollen from blossom to blossom.

RECYCLE: To recover something that has been thrown out and to use it in another way.

REPLANTING: Moving small plants from the containers the seeds were started in to a larger pot or an outdoor garden, to give the plants room to grow.

ROOT: The underground part of a plant that absorbs food and water from the soil.

ROOT VEGETABLES: Onions, potatoes, carrots, and other vegetables whose edible parts grow underground.

SHOOT: The young stem or branch of a plant.

SPADING FORK: A garden fork with flat tines, for digging and turning the soil.

STEM: The main stalk of a plant.

STERILE: Free from living things that can cause disease.

SUCCULENTS: Fleshy plants whose thick leaves and stems hold supplies of water.

THIN: To pull out some plants so that others will have room to grow.

TRENCH: A long cut in the soil.

VERMICULITE: A mineral material that will hold a great deal of water. It can be mixed with potting soil to start seeds in when gardening in pots.

VINE: A plant whose stem grows along the ground, like a pumpkin plant, or clings to a wall, like ivy.

WATERLOGGED: Completely soaked with water.

INDEX

4